1

turn

what do you call that?

Corn on the cob kiss!

HA.

5

Science is stuck to my sock... LIZ? can you get him off?

c'mon, Let go!

BITE

Ow!

I got bit!

aww, my socks got all streched out.

8

10

13

14

15

... the movie's over

...I know, I just didn't want anyone to see me crying.

aww. you cried at the end of "elf"? you're so cute.

SHHH!

17

18

20

21

22

23

25

26

27

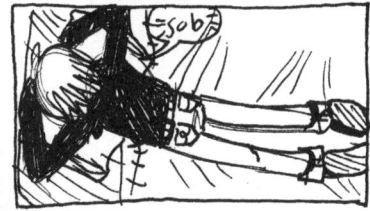

30

31

36

40

41

HI! How's tour going? I miss you.

it's ok. my battery is low, the phone might die, but I wanted to call because you're cute.

aw. was the show last night good? it was kinda sma...

...

hello?

darn.

50

57

66

LIZ

KOCHALKA
OCT 1, 2004